11.90

594   14.00   C.1
MAR   Martin, James.
            Tentacles.

	DATE DUE		

RENTON SCHOOL DISTRICT NO. 403

BRYN MAWR ELEM. SCHOOL
8212 South 118th Street
SEATTLE, WASH. 98178

TENTACLES

The Amazing World of Octopus, Squid, and Their Relatives

JAMES MARTIN

CROWN PUBLISHERS, INC., *New York*

Thanks to the folks at the Monterey Bay Aquarium
and the Seattle Aquarium.

Photographs on pages 16, 17, 20, 21 (top), 24 (top), 25, 27 (bottom), and
30 © Fred Bavendam; page 10 © Stephen Cooper; pages 1, 6 (right), 7, 14,
19, and 23 © Image Concepts/Jack and Sue Drafahl; pages 4 (bottom right),
9 (top), 12 (center), 13, and 15 © Thomas Kelly; pages 4 (center left and
right), 6 (center), 12 (top and bottom), and 31 © James Martin; pages 4
(top) and 26 by Robert F. Sisson, © 1967 National Geographic Society; page
4 (bottom left) © Kenneth R. H. Read; pages 8 and 21 (bottom) © Jeffrey L.
Rotman; pages 6 (left), 22, 24 (bottom), and 27 (top) © Sea Studios; page 9
(bottom) © David J. Wrobel.

Illustrations by Gaylord Welker

Published by Crown Publishers, Inc., a Random House company.
201 East 50th Street, New York, New York 10022
CROWN is a trademark of Crown Publishers, Inc.

Manufactured in the United States of America

Library of Congress Cataloging-in-Publication Data
Martin, James, 1950-
    Tentacles: the amazing world of octopus, squid, and their relatives / James Martin.
        p.   cm.
    Includes index.
    Summary: Introduces the defense mechanisms, reproduction, and other
characteristics of such cephalopods as the octopus, squid, nautilus, and cuttlefish.
    1. Cephalopoda—Juvenile literature. [1. Cephalopods.]
I. Title.
QL430.2.M37   1993
594'.5—dc20   92-22234

ISBN 0-517-59149-9 (trade)
        0-517-59150-2 (lib. bdg.)

10 9 8 7 6 5 4 3 2

*I*N 1872, a schooner was sailing on the Indian Ocean when two giant tentacles emerged from the water. Longer than any snake, they gripped the boat and pulled it below the surface. The water seemed to boil as more tentacles waved in the air. Sailors were dragged under. Over 100 witnesses saw the attack. None of the sailors survived.

The unlucky sailors were killed by a giant squid, a real-life sea monster. It may have mistaken their boat for its enemy, the sperm whale. Scientists have measured dead squid 70 feet in length, but they guess that the animals could grow to over 100 feet and weigh several tons. Giant squid usually live deep in the sea, thousands of feet below the surface, where no light penetrates. They float in darkness, waiting for unwary prey to swim into their tentacles.

▲ Giant squid

The giant squid possesses a frightening array of weapons. Large suckers dot its tentacles, giving it a powerful grip. Surrounding each sucker is a ring of sharp barbs that can cut through flesh for an even tighter hold. Many sperm whales are covered with scars from battles with giant squid.

As big as a man's fist, the giant squid's eyes are the largest eyes in the animal kingdom. Its beak is located in the center of its tentacles. It is sharp and curved, like a parrot's beak, and it moves from side to side, like scissors. The beak is tough and surrounded by powerful muscles. A giant squid can bite through steel cable.

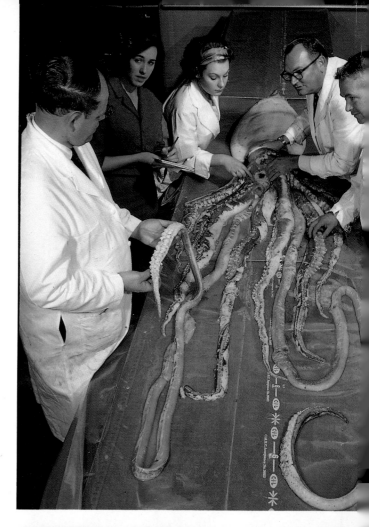

▲ Nautilus

▲ Cuttlefish

▲ Squid

▶ Octopus

◄ Scientists study a giant squid found off the coast of New-foundland in 1965. Because they spend most of their lives in deep water far from land, giant squid are very rarely seen. This one measured 21½ feet, including tentacles.

SCUBA DIVER, 6 feet

GREAT PACIFIC OCTOPUS, 8 feet

GIANT SQUID, 72 feet

SPERM WHALE, 68 feet

The giant squid is the largest member of the mollusk family, which includes sea slugs and garden snails, clams and oysters. Mollusks are *invertebrates*, animals without backbones or internal skeletons.

The smartest, strongest, fastest mollusks are the *cephalopods*: nautilus, cuttlefish, octopus, and squid. *Cephalopod* means "head-footed" (*cephalo*=head; *pod*=foot), a name they were given because tentacles grow out of their head.

Scientists divide cephalopods into two groups: the six species of nautilus, which have four gills, and all the others, 650 species of squid, octopus, and cuttlefish, which have two gills. Unlike most mollusks, which grow a hard shell for protection, most cephalopods have only an internal remnant of a shell. Only nautilus live inside a protective shell.

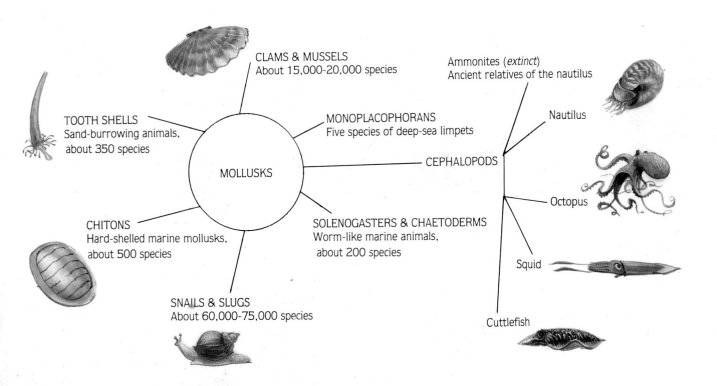

CLAMS & MUSSELS
About 15,000-20,000 species

Ammonites (*extinct*)
Ancient relatives of the nautilus

Nautilus

TOOTH SHELLS
Sand-burrowing animals,
about 350 species

MONOPLACOPHORANS
Five species of deep-sea limpets

MOLLUSKS

CEPHALOPODS

Octopus

CHITONS
Hard-shelled marine mollusks,
about 500 species

SOLENOGASTERS & CHAETODERMS
Worm-like marine animals,
about 200 species

Squid

SNAILS & SLUGS
About 60,000-75,000 species

Cuttlefish

All cephalopods have a circle of tentacles surrounding a hard beak. The rest of the animal is made up of a muscular sac, called the *mantle*, which contains the heart, brain, and other internal organs.

Tentacles are arms without bones. Squid and cuttlefish have ten tentacles—eight short and two long. Nautilus grow over 90 short ones. Octopus possess only eight. All species except the nautilus and a few rare squid have suckers on their tentacles. When food passes their way, the tentacles grab it and bring it to the beak.

MANTLE

EYE

FUNNEL

▼ A squid, with a semi-transparent mantle, short tentacles surrounding the mouth, and two long tentacles trailing behind.

▼ The suckers on the tentacles of a great Pacific octopus.

▼ An octopus's beak, surrounded by e suckered tentacles.

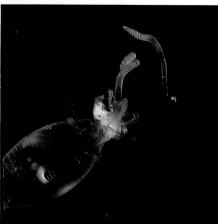

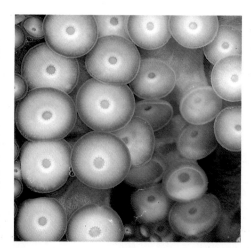

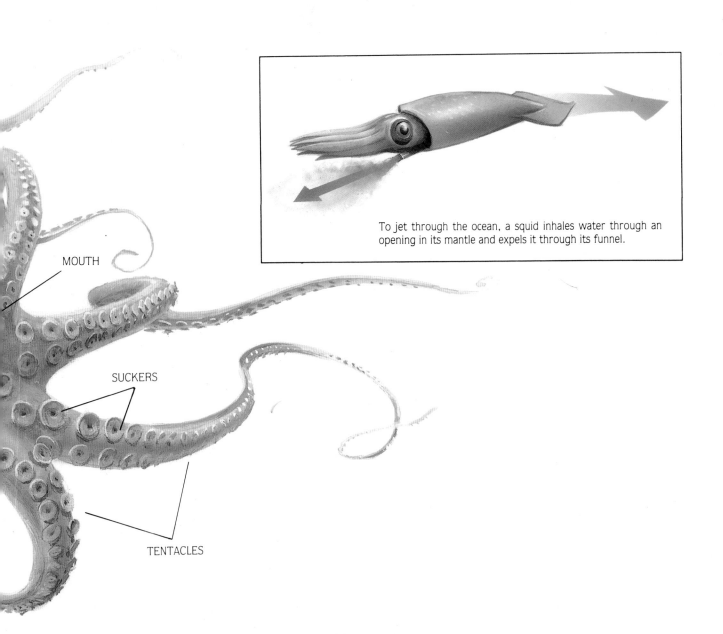

MOUTH

SUCKERS

TENTACLES

To jet through the ocean, a squid inhales water through an opening in its mantle and expels it through its funnel.

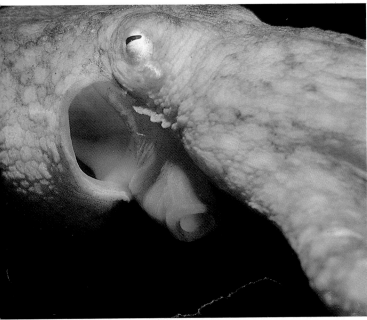

◀ Both mantle opening and funnel are visible below the eye of the octopus in this photograph.

Like fish, cephalopods use organs called *gills* to extract oxygen from the water. After the water passes across the gills, it is expelled through the *funnel*, or *siphon*. Cephalopods also use their funnels to propel themselves through the water. They inhale water and then force it out through the funnel by contracting the muscles of the mantle. They shoot backward like a released balloon.

▼ A small octopus changes from brick red to almost white.

Cephalopods are masters of deception and disguise. They change color with amazing speed, matching the background or making themselves transparent in an instant. Cuttlefish partially bury themselves and change to the color of sand. Octopus can alter the texture as well as the color of their skin to imitate rocks and sand.

The cephalopods that change color do so by expanding special color cells near the surface of their skin. These color cells are called *chromatophores*. Chromatophores are one of several different colors. To make a color appear on its skin, the animal flexes tiny strands of muscle surrounding only the chromatophores of that particular color. The chromatophores expand and the color appears. When the animal relaxes the muscles, that color disappears.

When threatened, most cephalopod species can shoot jets of ink. The ink not only hides the animal but, like an underwater stink bomb, confuses the enemy's sense of smell. Some squid are able to shoot ink in squid shapes. As the baffled predator attacks the ink squid, the real squid makes itself transparent and jets to safety.

All cephalopods lay eggs. Some species lay a few eggs, while others deposit thousands. Males fertilize the eggs by transferring capsules of sperm, called *spermatophores*, to the females. Soon after fertilization, the female lays her eggs. They hatch within a few weeks.

Although cephalopods share basic characteristics, their structures and survival tactics show amazing differences. Some depend on speed, others on stealth. Some dominate with great size, while others drift unseen in the dark.

▲ Octopus change their color, texture, and even shape to imitate their surroundings.

▼ Many octopus and squid can make themselves transparent. This octopus was found in Monterey Bay, California.

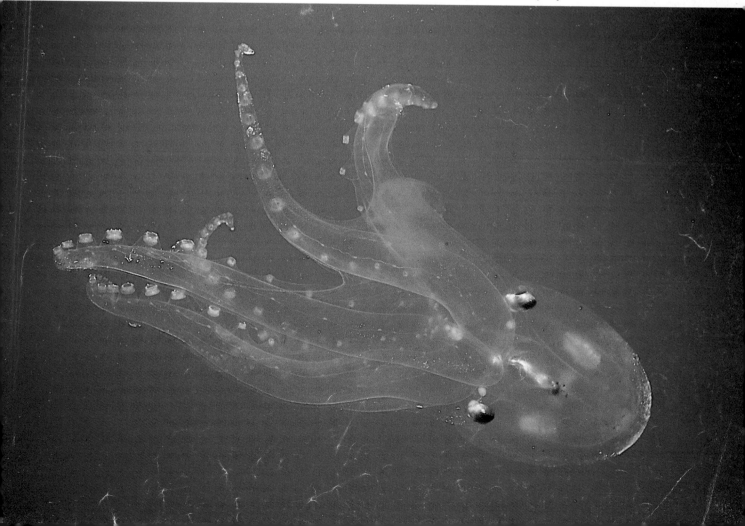

Nautilus

A

LIVING

FOSSIL

Five hundred and seventy million years ago, no fish swam in the sea. Worms, clam-like animals, and ancient relatives of the horseshoe crab called *trilobites* had the sea to themselves.

Then, about 500 million years ago, a frightening predator appeared in the ancient oceans. Encased in a shell, waving dozens of tentacles, and armed with a sharp beak, this predator pounced like a killer submarine. It was the first nautilus, a shelled cephalopod and the ancestor of today's octopus and squid. Some complete nautilus fossils from this era measure 10 feet across and fragments of others suggest they may have grown to 30 feet.

At first the ancient nautilus was king of the ocean. The other animals in the sea developed thicker shells to defend themselves against the killer beak, but no animal could fight a nautilus and win. Then, as the ages passed, new species developed with the tools to defeat the nautilus's defenses. Fish with powerful jaws were able to crush the nautilus's shell. Some dinosaurs dove into the sea to feast on the slow-moving nautilus.

To avoid predators, the nautilus learned to go deep, where it was too dark for fish to see it and too deep for diving reptiles. It visited the food-rich surface of the sea to feed only on moonless nights, when its enemies couldn't see it.

At one time, 2,500 nautilus species roamed the sea. Today, only six types survive, unchanged from their original forms. Known as "chambered nautilus," they live where the Indian and South Pacific oceans meet. When the moon wanes, they still bob to the surface to feed on shrimp, small fish, and other prey in darkness and safety, just as their ancient ancestors did.

▼ Some ancient nautilus species had a straight shell instead of the curled shell of modern nautilus. This one is from a group called *orthoceratids*, which had a shell up to 12 feet long.

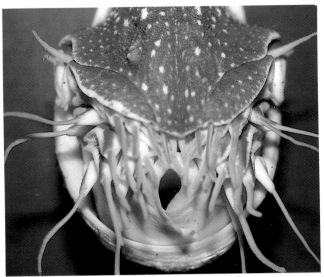

▲ This front view shows the nautilus's tentacles and funnel (*in the center*).

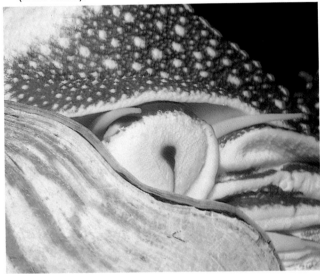

▲ Closeup of a nautilus's eye.

▲ Closeup of a nautilus's shell.

While the size and structure of squid and octopus vary widely, all nautilus look alike. Over 90 tentacles wave in front of dark, pitted eyes. The shell grows in a spiral, like a snail's shell, and colored stripes decorate the surface.

The animal gets its name from the chambers in its shell. The nautilus fills each chamber with gas to change its buoyancy. More gas makes the nautilus lighter, so it bobs upward; with less gas, it sinks. By regulating buoyancy, the nautilus doesn't waste energy swimming to change depth.

As the nautilus grows, it adds chambers. The shell spirals ever larger, reaching as much as one foot across. The animal itself lives in the most recently grown chamber.

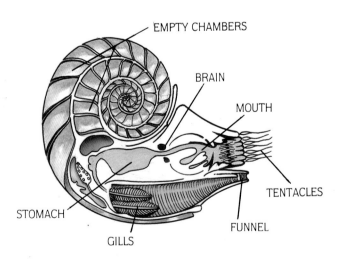

EMPTY CHAMBERS

BRAIN

MOUTH

TENTACLES

FUNNEL

GILLS

STOMACH

▲ A cross section of a nautilus, showing the chambers of its shell. The animal's organs are in the last chamber, nearest the opening.

Nautilus mate face to face, tentacles tangled together. After the male transfers the spermatophore, the female lays about a dozen large, thick-shelled eggs up to 1,000 feet below the surface of the ocean. One year later, the young nautilus emerge from the shells fully formed—miniature replicas of their parents.

Unlike its relatives the squid and octopus, the nautilus cannot change color or create a cloud of ink. Its eye has no lens for focusing, so nautilus can only see vague shapes. The tentacles touch and taste, but they have no suckers to help hold on to prey.

Instead of a firm tube, the nautilus's funnel consists of two flaps. The animal can't direct water with much force. The hard shell protects, but it also decreases mobility. As a result, the nautilus moves in a slow and relatively clumsy way, bobbing like a soggy underwater cork.

Since the nautilus first appeared on earth, thousands of species have come and gone. Nowhere on earth can you find a dinosaur or a mastodon. Giant sloths are gone. You need not worry about saber-toothed tigers or eurypterids, six-foot-long killer insects, anymore. But the nautilus still hunts in the South Pacific Ocean, a living fossil.

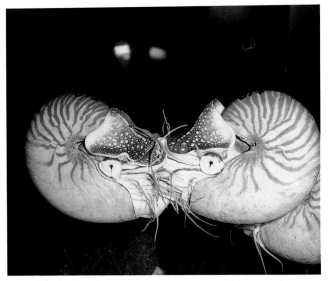

▲ Nautilus mating.

▲ Baby nautilus.

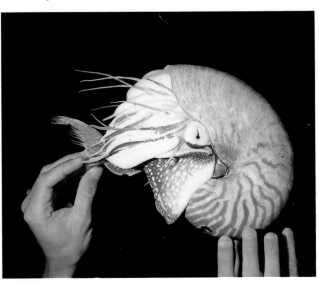

▲ Adult nautilus.

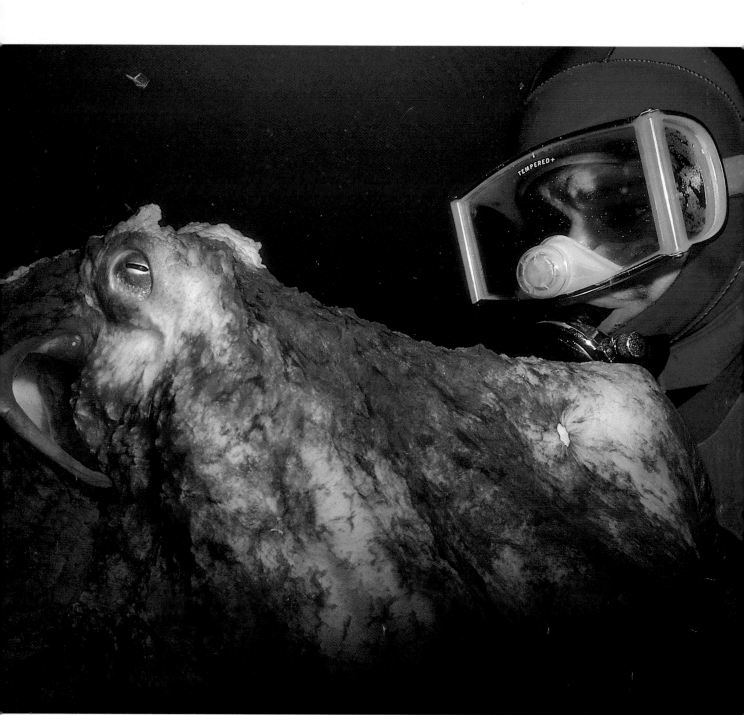

Octopus

THE ESCAPE ARTIST

In Puget Sound near Seattle, scuba divers sometimes notice that the sea floor is watching them. Something the color and texture of the surrounding rocks lies still, with only a dark eye betraying its presence.

The eye belongs to the great Pacific octopus. At 150 pounds in weight and eight feet across, it is one of the largest octopus species.

Like all octopus, the great Pacific octopus can raise its eyes above its body like periscopes, peeking over rocks without giving away its position. The skin housing the eyes bubbles out of the body like someone blowing gum.

Because the octopus has no skeleton, its body is not rigid. An octopus is like a bag of water surrounded by eight tentacles. The skin flows, changing shape and texture moment by moment. An octopus can pour itself through a hole the size of an orange.

When threatened, octopus squirt ink to conceal their flight. They head for the sea floor, where their skin mimics the color and texture of rocks or mud. This color change occurs in an instant, sometimes with the skin surface stippled like giant goose bumps.

Octopus wear their feelings on their skin. When angry or frightened, the skin on many species turns brick red, returning to shades of gray and tan when the animal grows calm.

Their wonderful skin injures easily. Octopus allow divers to pet them sometimes, but a rough glove can tear their skin.

The octopus's fluid body allows it to raise its eyes above its body. . . .

and to flow through holes and narrow openings.

Octopus can jet through the water with their funnel, but they usually crawl on the sea floor looking for food, using their tentacles like legs. Most species live near the shore and prefer to hide in the daylight and hunt in the dark, when they cannot be seen by either predators or prey. They recognize food in the dark by tasting with their suckers. Imagine moving through a darkened kitchen with tongues on your fingertips.

When hunting in daylight, some octopus surprise prey by floating down from above. The skin between the tentacles stretches thin and billows like a parachute.

When the octopus finds a meal such as a clam, it grips the shell with its suckers and pulls it apart. Even a small octopus has a powerful grip: it takes a 40-pound pull to break the grip of a three-pound octopus.

A rasping tongue, called a *radula*, saws through the shell. The radula is spoon-shaped and covered with rows of sharp teeth. With it, the octopus injects poisonous saliva into the clam. The poison causes the muscles to relax. The octopus overturns the clam, snipping the meat from the shell with its beak.

▼ In addition to eating live animals, such as crabs and clams, octopus are scavengers. Here a great Pacific octopus feeds on the dead body of a spiny dogfish.

Generally, the smaller the octopus, the more poisonous its bite. Every year people die from the surprisingly painless bite of the tiny, fist-sized blue-ringed octopus of Indonesia and Australia.

Smaller species tend to act more aggressively, too. Larger octopus tend to be shy and gentle. Although much stronger than a man, an octopus, unless cornered, will flee rather than fight. Dangerous encounters with octopus usually happen when something attracts the curious creature. Tentacles grab a shiny wrist watch or face mask. If the octopus refuses to release its prize, the diver could run out of air and die.

Octopus are a favorite food for seals, sharks, and eels. Moray eels hide on the sea bottom and strike at the root of the octopus's tentacles with their muscular jaws. The eels spin in the water, tearing the tentacle from the octopus, who swims away quickly to hide and recover. In time, it will grow a new tentacle; sometimes the new tentacle will sprout several smaller tentacles at its tip. An octopus that loses only a tentacle can count itself lucky. Hungry sharks and seals seldom allow their prey to escape.

▼ A female blue-ringed octopus. The bulbous orange objects she is carrying are eggs. Unlike most octopus species, which lay their eggs in dens (*see pages 20-21*), the female blue-ringed octopus carries her eggs with her.

Aquarium keepers mistrust the octopus. Their intelligence, curiosity, and fluidity make them escape experts. Even a big octopus can squeeze through a narrow slit atop an aquarium. Sometimes, keepers line the top of their aquariums with strips of Astroturf, hoping the rough material will irritate the octopus's tender skin and discourage escape. But an octopus bent on escape is a determined animal, and Astroturf often fails to stop them.

Once out of the aquarium, the escapee can travel a long way on land before lack of water suffocates it. Jacques Cousteau reported that an octopus kept in a friend's home aquarium escaped one day. It was found in the library, pulling down books and paging through them.

Octopus appear to recognize individual divers and keepers. At the Seattle Aquarium, an octopus tormented one keeper. Whenever she passed his tank, he would pull himself out of the water, aim his funnel, and hit her with a blast of water. Another octopus, named Thor, insisted that all who passed say, "Hello, Thor." Anyone who failed to greet him was hosed from behind. Underwater, wild octopus hide from strangers but will allow divers they know to play with them.

Octopus learn by watching. In one experiment, scientists placed an octopus in a tank with two balls. One ball hid a snack. After several tries, the octopus learned to look for the snack behind the correct ball. Meanwhile, the scientists allowed another octopus to watch. The second octopus learned the trick just by watching and went to the ball that hid the snack on the first try.

▲ A female great Pacific octopus guards her eggs, which are hanging in strings from the roof of her den.

Octopus live in dens among the rocks on the sea bottom. They improve these natural nooks by building walls at the entrance with bits of stone and shell. They also use bottles, cans, and other litter when available. Octopus are attracted by shiny things like glass and metal.

A female octopus lays thousands of eggs—as many as 50,000 in as little as two weeks. She hangs strings of the eggs at the entrance to her den, washing them with water to prevent fungus attack and shooing away fish hoping to make a meal of them. As she guards the eggs, waiting for the young to hatch, she does not eat. Like a mother salmon, she is at the end of her life cycle. After the eggs hatch, she will die.

The baby octopus are surrounded by a clear, jelly-like shell. After about 50 days, they hatch. Most species emerge from the eggs looking like miniature adults, but some pass through a larval stage, like a caterpillar before it becomes a butterfly. The young octopus float among the plankton at the surface of the sea. The plankton fields provide food, but they also attract animals with a taste for young octopus. Of the thousands that hatch, only a very few—perhaps no more than a dozen—will grow to maturity.

▶ A newborn great Pacific octopus (*lower right*), surrounded by a cluster of white eggs.

▼ Baby octopus and diver in the Red Sea.

Squid

THE UNDERWATER MISSILE

Most invertebrates move slowly. Without bones to pull against, their muscles have little leverage. Try to imagine moving your hand to your shoulder without any bones in your arm. The contracting muscles would merely shorten your arm, not bend it. Without bones, a human being would merely twitch, like a bowl of jelly.

Squid have transformed the lack of a skeleton into an advantage. They move like living missiles. Instead of pushing against water with fins like a fish, they inhale water, thereby stretching the muscles of the mantle. When the muscles contract, water squeezes through the funnel. The funnel acts like a jet engine, blasting water behind. The squid's narrow shape allows it to speed through the water with little resistance. Thin fins along their sides help to steer. When the squid is moving slowly, these fins ripple like an eel's, allowing it to hover in the water.

One species, the flying squid, creates enough force with its funnel to leap out of the water. It extends its fins and glides like a flying squirrel. It can glide for over 50 feet. Sometimes it lands on the deck of a boat, surprising those aboard.

With more than 375 species, squid are the most numerous cephalopods. They live in all ocean environments, from cold, dark water more than a mile deep to warm tropical reefs near the surface. The smallest and largest cephalopods are squid, ranging from only three-quarters of an inch to over 70 feet.

◀ Squid swarming to mate in the sea near California's Channel Islands (*see page 25*).

▼ A closeup of the eye and delicately patterned skin of a squid.

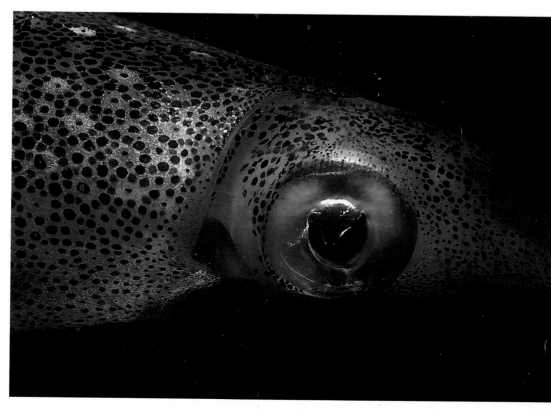

▲ A group of southern calamary squid, photographed near the Australian coast. The squid's streamlined shape enables it to jet through the water at high speed.

Unlike the shy and gentle octopus, most squid are aggressive predators. They prowl the sea like jet fighters, sometimes hunting in schools and following migrations of the fish they like to eat. Most species of squid possess all the weapons of the giant squid on a smaller scale: "toothed" suckers, a sharp beak, and grasping tentacles.

▲ The squid's beak is in the center of its ten suckered tentacles.

Six-foot-long Humboldt squid hunt in packs, like wolves. Unlike wolves, however, they don't cooperate or use strategy to capture their prey. Instead, they attack all at once, with several squid tugging at the victim at the same time. While large fish are their usual victims, Humboldts have occasionally attacked divers. Survivors tell of tentacles being wrapped around them, of barbed suckers cutting their skin, and of being dragged down by the powerful animals.

Dozens of creatures eat squid: from whales, sharks, and cod to seals and penguins. Scientists have counted hundreds of undigested squid beaks in the stomach of one sperm whale. Predators gather in areas where squid swarm to mate, such as the shallow water near California's Channel Islands. There, for two days each November, seals and sharks plow through the ocean with their mouths open, feeding on the swarms of mating squid.

▼ Many animals feed on squid. Here a flounder eats a boreal squid.

Like octopus, squid can change color. Many species also glow in the dark. This is called *bioluminescence*, which means "living light." Deep-water squid have light-producing organs, called *photophores*, in their skin. Photophores glow when two chemicals, called *luciferin* and *luciferase*, react together, producing a blue-green light. The light is colored and scattered by lenses in the photophores. Reds, blues, greens, and whites sparkle in the darkness. The squid use their light to lure prey and to communicate with other squid. Thousands of feet below the surface, where no light penetrates, bioluminescence works better than posturing, camouflage, and color change.

Other species of bioluminescent squid live near the surface. Instead of chemicals, many of these squid use colonies of glowing bacteria to create light. The bacteria live just under the squid's skin. This arrangement benefits both the squid and the bacteria: the squid uses the lights for hunting and communicating, and the bacteria have a place to live. One Mediterranean squid has an unusual use for bioluminescence: when attacked, it discharges a cloud of glowing bacteria instead of ink. It escapes as the puzzled predator concentrates on the lights.

◄ A photograph taken under ultraviolet light reveals a bright patch of bioluminescence on the mantle of this squid.

Squid lay clusters of clear eggs. The female attaches the cluster, which contains several hundred eggs, to the sea floor or to another cluster. Soon the sea floor looks like a forest of egg clusters.

After depositing her eggs, the female loses strength and dies. Crabs and other scavengers pick at the remains of the dead squid. They leave the eggs alone, because the egg cases are covered with a nasty-tasting goo. But when the eggs hatch, the baby squid become easy meals for many sea creatures.

▲ A newly hatched squid. The mantle is on the left, the dark eyes and developing tentacles on the right.

▼ Reef squid laying their eggs among sea grasses off the coast of New Guinea.

The deep is home to the strangest squid. In the dark, cold world half a mile below the surface lurk species with bodies that are as soft as gelatin. The intense pressure at that depth would kill a human instantly, but these animals are comfortable there. They float with the currents, snatching any food that passes their way.

The 70-foot-long giant squid spends most of its life drifting in the cool, dark currents 2,000 or more feet below the surface of the Atlantic and Pacific oceans. Its smaller relative, the jeweled squid, has a transparent body, but its skin sparkles. Twenty-two light organs housed in ten different structures on its mantle make it one of the most brilliant deep-sea creatures. Another strange species, the sail squid, has a left eye that sticks out like a gourd and can approach one third the size of its head. Its other eye is of normal size. No one knows why.

▲ The jeweled squid has a transparent mantle and 22 photophores that produce light in several different colors.

▲ The vampire squid gets its name from the cape-like membrane joining its tentacles. It has large red eyes and two horn-like fins on its mantle.

◄ The body of this sail squid is covered with photophores. Strangest of all, its left eye is bigger than its right eye.

Another deep-sea species, the vampire squid, gets its name from the web of skin it has between its tentacles, which resembles Dracula's cape. Two fins sprout from its head like devilish horns. The vampire squid is a "missing link": its bulbous body resembles that of an octopus, but its internal anatomy is a squid's, and scientists note its similarities to the ancient ancestors of both squid and octopus. The vampire squid can be found between 1,000 and 6,000 feet deep. It has giant red eyes and glows in the dark. Like the nautilus, the vampire squid hasn't changed in hundreds of millions of years.

It is hard for scientists to study fast-moving squid jetting near the surface or floating out of sight in the depths. Unlike other cephalopods, they die quickly in aquariums. Although squid are common, we know little about them. The most common cephalopod remains the most mysterious.

Cuttlefish

THE
QUICK-CHANGE
ARTIST

When a cuttlefish is hunting, cascades of swirling color—gold, blue, brown, and silver—flow over its skin, which is striped like a zebra's. It moves slowly, using its fins and gentle jets of water to approach its prey. Then two tentacles shoot out to grab the victim and pull it toward the cuttlefish's hard jaws.

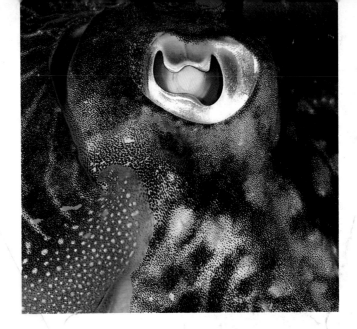

◄ A giant cuttlefish. Although most cuttlefish only reach one foot, this species can grow to six feet in length.

▶ A closeup of the eye and fantastically patterned skin of a common cuttlefish.

Cuttlefish are quick-change artists. Their skins change color and pattern at dizzying speed. Even when they are at rest, subtle color shifts wash over them. Color serves several purposes. Cuttlefish seem to use color to hypnotize their prey. It is also a visual language other cuttlefish understand. One set of patterns may suggest a willingness to mate, while another pattern means "stay away." And color provides camouflage: cuttlefish match their background as they lie half-buried on the sea floor while waiting for a meal to swim by or hiding from their enemies.

Cuttlefish have a chambered internal shell called a "cuttlebone." Like the nautilus, they regulate their buoyancy by filling the chambers with gas.

Cuttlefish look like squat squid. Thin fins run along their sides and ten tentacles emerge from their heads, although they usually keep the two longest tentacles retracted in a pouch beneath their eyes. Few cuttlefish exceed one foot in length. Most live in the eastern Atlantic or the Indo-Pacific near Australia and Indonesia. A few species venture into the Mediterranean, but none live off the coasts of the Americas.

There are two groups of cuttlefish, the *Sepia* and the smaller *Sepiola*. For centuries, the dark writing ink called "sepia" came from the ink sacs of cuttlefish.

When looking for a mate, the male performs a complex dance of movement and color change. If the female agrees to mate, they face each other and weave their tentacles together. A few hours later she lays her eggs. The eggs are each about half an inch long and are laid in spiral coils.

Like their relatives the squid and the octopus, cuttlefish are prized for their meat. In fact, most people know cephalopods only as food—or from myths and stories about sea monsters. But scientists are beginning to unlock the secrets of their behavior. A group of animals we once considered alien and frightening is proving to be intelligent and wonderfully adapted to their environment.

GLOSSARY

bioluminescence The production of light by an animal, either chemically or with glowing bacteria.

cephalopod A mollusk with tentacles and a hard beak. Most can change color and use ink for defense.

chromatophore A color cell.

funnel A tube-like organ used by cephalopods for locomotion. The animal squeezes water through the funnel to jet through the sea. Also called the *siphon*.

gill An underwater version of a lung that absorbs oxygen from water for respiration.

invertebrate An animal without a backbone.

mantle The muscular sheath surrounding the internal organs of a cephalopod.

mollusk An invertebrate with skin that secretes mucus. Its body is often protected by a shell.

photophore A light-emitting organ.

plankton Tiny animals and plants that drift in the ocean currents. They are an important source of food for larger sea animals.

radula The rasping tongue of a mollusk.

spermatophore A capsule of sperm transferred by the male to the female with a specially adapted tentacle.

INDEX